Harold and Joan

Life Before We Got Modern

Harold and Joan

Life Before We Got Modern

ALISON DEAR

Copyright © 2020 Alison Dear

The moral right of the author has been asserted.

Apart from any fair dealing for the purposes of research or private study, or criticism or review, as permitted under the Copyright, Designs and Patents Act 1988, this publication may only be reproduced, stored or transmitted, in any form or by any means, with the prior permission in writing of the publishers, or in the case of reprographic reproduction in accordance with the terms of licences issued by the Copyright Licensing Agency. Enquiries concerning reproduction outside those terms should be sent to the publishers.

Matador
9 Priory Business Park,
Wistow Road, Kibworth Beauchamp,
Leicestershire, LE8 0RX
Tel: 0116 279 2299
Email: books@troubador.co.uk
Web: www.troubador.co.uk/matador
Twitter: @matadorbooks

ISBN 978 183859 306 3

British Library Cataloguing in Publication Data.
A catalogue record for this book is available from the British Library.

Printed and bound by CPI Group (UK) Ltd, Croydon, CR0 4YY
Typeset in 12pt Adobe Garamond Pro by Troubador Publishing Ltd, Leicester, UK

Matador is an imprint of Troubador Publishing Ltd

For Harold and Joan
Mum and Dad

Thanks to my husband Graham, for proof reading, suggestions and cups of coffee.

Contents

Foreword	ix
Who's who?	xii
Here for ages	1
One village – one family	4
Another village family	11
Utilities and facilities	17
Outbreak	21
Evacuation	24
The war effort	27
Rationing	30
School	33
War news	39
Crash	41
Fun and games	44

The end	47
After the end	49
A new start	53
Heading into the modern age with added snow	59
The great escape – cars for all	65
Last thoughts	67
Afterword	71

Foreword

In the South East of Gloucestershire, not quite in Wiltshire, not quite in Oxfordshire, sits the Cotswold village of Ampney Crucis. Before the arrival of the internet and the 'find address' function, it was a name that I spelt out slowly in telephone conversations on at least a weekly basis. "Yes Ampney Crucis. That's ay em pee, enn ee why, then a new word, see are you, see, yes that's right see, eye, ess. No I don't know if the pee is meant to be silent but most people say just say amnee… yes it does look a bit like circus but it's croosis."

I was born in Ampney Crucis, so was my dad. So was his mum and her mum and a few more mums and dads before that. His ancestors were some of the first pupils at the village school, that began began educating the local youth almost half a century before Captain Cook landed in Australia in 1770. My grandparents took their first steps in the Edwardian era and their teenage years had the backdrop of the First World War. This war has moved into history and now the Second World War is also moving backwards in time. There is a vast library of records, chronicling the years between 1939 and 1945, but the overwhelming majority relate to adults: soldiers, wives, mothers, land girls, munition workers, Bevan boys and conscientious objectors have all been the subject of books, films and TV documentaries. One group of children, the evacuees, began to have their voices heard relatively recently as have those children who experienced the Blitz. But another group of children feature less in these archives, and these are the children of the countryside who stayed at home. For this group of children, war did not bring upheaval and destruction but a quite different experience. There were, of course, individual tragedies, the four names inscribed at the foot of the village war memorial were husbands, fathers, sons and brothers. However, for many children in rural communities, war brought opportunities for never experienced excitement.

Our dad, Harold, was one of those children. Beginning in 2017 we talked and taped all the stories that my sisters and I had heard a fair few times before and some that we had not. We talked, not just about the war, but village life in the 1930s and before, as well as the villagers, including family members, who were part of that life. Our mum, Joan, joined in with her memories of Ampney Crucis in the early 1950s when she arrived as a new bride from North Yorkshire and

Foreword

they both described the changes of the 1960s. I have just added information and context for readers less familiar with the village and these times.

So this is Harold and Joan: life before we got modern.

Who's who?

Anyone who has researched their family history, and then attempted to give the information to other family members, will have experienced the problem of relationship name changes depending on the audience.

"That's my dad, your grandad… Your cousin, that's my aunt." Rather than using a mass of explanatory brackets, there follows a much pruned tree, showing Dad's direct ancestors and, in bold, the names that they are referred to throughout. Hopefully, it will make for easier reading.

Who's who?

Some twigs on the family tree

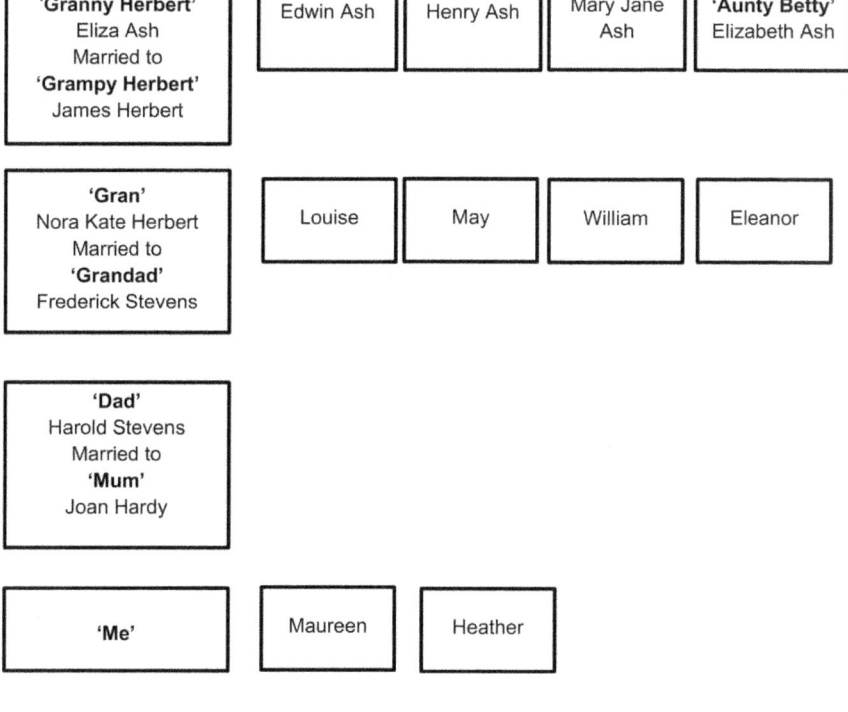

Here for ages

A quick glance at a map shows Ampney Crucis sitting around three miles from the town of Cirencester. During Roman times this town was known as Corinium, and, as I imagine all local school children are still informed, second only to London/Londinium in importance. The name of the village that causes so much difficulty, stems from two sources. Ampney is thought to come from the Latin for stream that runs along the bottom of the village, the troublesome 'Crucis' relates to the fifteenth century cross in the churchyard. Two other Ampneys lie close by: Ampney St Peter and Ampney St Mary. Both take their names from their churches but in the 1930s they were known locally as Easington and Ashbrook – Dad still refers to them by these names. About half a mile from Ampney Crucis is Hilcot End, this hamlet of around fifteen houses is a place in its own right, but at the time, was very much considered

Definitely not to scale! Ampney Crucis within the county of Gloucestershire.

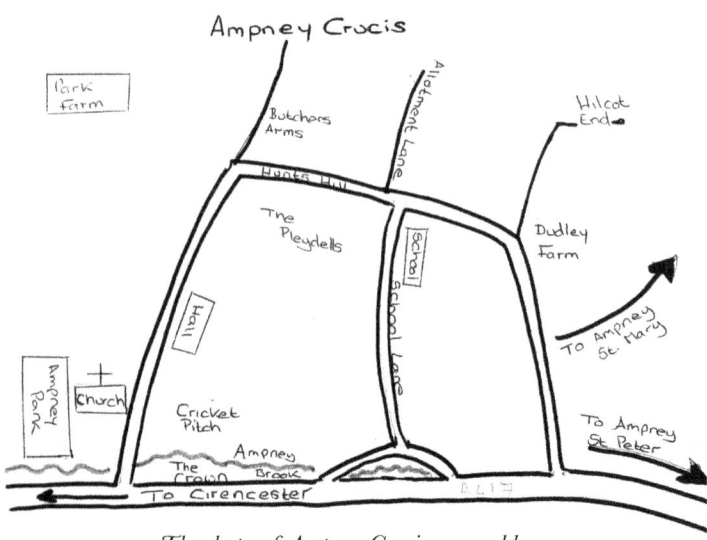

The shape of Ampney Crucis… roughly…

as part of the Ampneys. Although the distances by road to any of the three larger villages would now be usually completed by car, in the 1930s it was the much shorter distances of footpaths through the fields that joined the four settlements together.

The main village of Ampney Crucis is, very roughly, rectangular. The bottom side is now the A417 which runs alongside Ampney brook. The left and the top sides are peppered with a variety of houses, both old and new, while the right hand side running back to the main road has just a few houses, and is the border between Ampney Crucis and the smaller Ampney St Mary. The rectangle is bisected by 'School Lane' which leads back to the brook.

Although many of the houses are less than one hundred years old, there has not been a significant increase in the number of people living in the village. The population of Ampney Crucis in 2016 was 636, barely one hundred more than the 1901 population of 524.

One village – one family

Today, the Cotswolds is one of the wealthiest parts of the county and the country. In Ampney Crucis, the majority of houses are owner occupied and, sitting writing this in the summer of 2018, they are commanding some eye-watering prices in the rare event of one coming onto the market. When I was growing up in the 1970s, these extraordinary prices and the social change that came with them had yet to materialise but there were glimpses of what was to come. In the 1930s this transformation was unimaginable.

The idea of a 'Lord of the Manor' might be thought of as one belonging to the era of Jane Austen and it is true that in general, by the time Dad was born, the power of the local squire was fading. The work opportunities of the First World War had ended the idea of a life of domestic service as being the only option for many working women. Men had arrived back from the front with a greater awareness of the differences in opportunity between the 'haves' and 'have nots'. But real change was still around the corner and throughout the 1930s, as in three decades before, Ampney Crucis was dominated by one family of 'haves': the Cripps.

The family had been associated with Cirencester for many years but in the late 1890s acquired Ampney Park. This is a large house next to the church but hidden from view by a large stone wall, sections of which are occasionally demolished by errant HGVs. If in 2018 you had no other use for nine million pounds, then this house and its gardens could have been yours. Although not on the scale of some other estates, in the late 1800s servants comfortably outnumbered family. The 1891 census listed the head of the family being Edmund Cripps with his wife Ada and their four children Frederick, Egerton, Gwendoline and Eleanor, looked after by ladies maids, housemaids, kitchen maids, a footman, and a cook. The servants were English with one exception as the education of the children was entrusted to a governess from Switzerland, one Albertina Wurmli. Albertina seems to have replaced the original governess, Cirencester born Edith Jones.

Edmund died in the 1890s and so in 1901 his widow Ada was head of the Ampney Park household with her second son, the unusually named Egerton Tymewell. Egerton was occupied as a brewery director along with the newly married heir to the estate Frederick, who was living in Coxwell Street in Cirencester with his wife Constance. Although these two people were yet to have children, they still required the services of a butler, a cook, two housemaids and a kitchen maid. Ada was still head of Ampney Park in 1911 but in the intervening years Frederick had moved to Waterton House, less than a mile from the family HQ, with Constance, their four children and nine servants. Frederick appears to have felt there were benefits to his Swiss education delivered by Ms Wurmli as his children's governess, Margot Salchlie, hailed from Berne.

After Ada's death, the estate passed to the heir, Frederick, and the 1939 record shows the family arrangement remembered by Dad. Frederick and Constance were now in their 60s and living at Ampney Park and were a constant presence in the lives of the villagers.

"The Cripps basically controlled the village. You worked for them, or someone in your family did, they more than likely owned your house. If you talked about them it was always 'Sir Frederick' and 'Lady Cripps'. Mostly the villagers were employed for farm work, everything was manual labour especially the harvest. It was still mostly horses then, they had six horses and two tractors. New workers or temporary workers might need to be given accommodation and if your house was thought to be the most suitable, well, you were just moved. I think Granny Herbert,

lived in just about every house in Hilcot End because she was moved that often and she also lived in Ampney Crucis as well. She was in a little cottage in School Lane by about 1914. Your grandad didn't work for the Cripps but your gran was a seamstress for them and they also owned their cottage.

The Cripps' estate used to be huge before the First War, right from Ready Token right up to the Whiteway on the Stow road. They didn't just have Ampney Park, they owned Waterton House as well. But by the '30s it was quite a bit smaller. Rumour had it that they had investments in Krupp Armaments and they lost their money in the First World War."

Krupp Armaments were a German engineering company who had worked with British companies in the Victorian and Edwardian times. This changed in the First World War, when they became a major supplier of the equipment mowing down soldiers from Great Britain and the Commonwealth, while Vickers, the British equivalent, provided the opposition. After 1914, I can't imagine German companies were sending share dividends to the Cotswolds and this might have contributed to the Cripps' decision to sell part of their estate.

The influence of the Germans might seem strange given that both Frederick and Egerton saw active service throughout the First World War; Frederick was awarded the DSO having served in France from 1916 and Egerton

A glimpse of Ampney Park from the churchyard.

the MC after a campaign that included the Dardanelles and Gaza. However, the family connection to Germany stemmed back to the Victorian age when in 1884 Wilfred Cripps, brother of Edmund, the first Cripps owner of Ampney Park, married his second wife Helena. Helena Augusta Wilhelmine Bismark, to give her her full name, was the daughter of Count Bismark of Schierstein. The Count was a relative of the chancellor Otto von Bismark who at one time was much admired by Queen Victoria's grandson, Wilhelm the second, better known as Kaiser Bill. This gentleman's fractious relationship with his various cousins contributed the deaths of over sixteen million people in the First World War.

The description of the Cripps might seem to paint them as villains – living in luxury and treating the whole village as 'theirs' but Dad described how this was simply the system of the time and they were more appreciated than resented.

> *"The Cripps, they were very good to the village, people in the village thought well of them. At that time, families like them understood that, as they practically owned the village, they had a duty towards it and the people who lived there as it was their village as well. When I was a kid you could go anywhere on the estate, it wasn't a case of having to stick to footpaths because it was someone else's land. If you wanted to walk across a grass field to*

get somewhere you could, if you wanted to go and play somewhere you could. They did practical things as well, they provided facilities in the village such as the village hall and if something like the cemetery was looking untidy they would send men to sort it out. They also assisted the villagers in emergency situations, I remember there was a terrible winter in 1946 and they sent men to clear a track through the village otherwise everyone would have been snowed in their houses for weeks."

So there were benefits, but they came with clear, if unspoken, requirements in return.

"But they were very powerful, you had to toe the line and not rock the boat. I can remember that a couple of teenagers were messing around with an air rifle and shot a hole in the radiator of one of their tractors. It was agreed that the best thing they could do was to go into the army. Although nothing would have been said, the family would have known that if the boys had refused the family could simply have been asked to leave the village."

Another village family

The Cripps might have had the power but our family had the numbers. Gran was the youngest of five children and her mother was Eliza, always referred to as Granny Herbert. Born in 1866, Granny Herbert was the fourth child of villagers James Ash and Harriet Ayres. In the 1901 census, of the population of 524, just under ten per cent of the villagers had the surname Herbert, Ash or Ayres. No doubt the number of married daughters meant that the real total would have been far higher.

Most of the Herbert family lived out their lives in Ampney Crucis and the surrounding villages, working on farms and in the mills, but there were a few exceptions. Granny Herbert's brother Henry emigrated to America in 1862, where he set up a plumbing business in Boston with some of his cousins. Early in 1914 unemployment forced her only son William, Gran's brother, to join them. The only female who moved away was Granny Herbert's younger sister Elizabeth or 'Aunty Betty'. By the age of twenty-three, perhaps after deciding that marrying a village boy and staying in Ampney Crucis for the rest of her life was not for her, she was working in London as a parlour maid for John Collyer, a barrister in Paddington. She spent the rest of her life in London and Surrey but returned regularly to Ampney Crucis for visits.

> *"Aunty Betty, the sister who went to London, I remember visiting them in London just before the war. She always had a bit more of everything. She married twice and one of her husbands was an insurance man. That sort of job would have been quite a step up moneywise compared to marrying a farm worker. Aunty Betty had these black beads, great lengths of them, I don't know what they were made of, I suppose they were just glass but even so they would have been more of a luxury item."*

Meanwhile, her older sister Eliza married James Herbert, a local boy, and became 'Granny Herbert'. Photographs show a capable looking woman with very consistent headwear.

> *"Granny Herbert always wore this great big black hat shaped like a coal scuttle. She wore it wherever she went and kept it black by giving it a coat of paint every year. Grampy Herbert worked at Coles Mill and as well as that, the place they had in Hilcot End*

Another village family

*A host of Herberts. Granny Herbert and
Aunty Betty front row with signature hat and beads.*

*was a sort of pub or off-licence. But it wasn't a pub in
the way way they are today it was used almost as an
official building, I know inquests were held there."*

I was always aware that Gran was the youngest of Granny Herbert's five children but that the others had died. Other than that we seemed to know very little about them and it felt that even their names were becoming 'lost'. The internet revealed Gran's sisters as Louise, May and Eleanor. In seven years between 1912 and 1919 all three sisters married and had children but in almost the same length of time all three died of tuberculosis: May in 1915, Louise in 1916 and finally Eleanor in 1921. William, now Gran's only sibling, had already emigrated to America and fought in the First World War with the American army. He returned to England briefly and married a local girl, Margaret Tanner, before returning to Boston in 1921 only to die just three years later aged thirty. Granny Herbert, meanwhile, was bringing up four grandchildren with the help of Gran, her only surviving daughter, long before the arrival of the welfare state. There certainly wouldn't have been spare money for new hats.

Granny and Grampy Herbert both lived to see their granddaughters act as bridesmaids to Gran, always known as Kitty. She married Fred Stevens in 1931 and they became 'Gran and Grandad'. They moved into number 37 Ampney Crucis and lived there for the rest of their lives.

Spring 1931. Photographs in the garden after the wedding of Gran and Grandad.

Utilities and facilities

Gran in the 1920s.

Number 37 Ampney Crucis.

A new arrival at number 37 – Dad with Gran.

Harold and Joan: Life Before We Got Modern

Believed to be Gran's only brother, William, who emigrated to Boston and fought with the American Army in the First World War..

Utilities and facilities

Broadband arrived in Ampney Crucis a few years ago but gas has never made it. In the 1930s electricity had turned up with the electricity board supplying each house with one socket. Mains water and sewerage were way in the future.

Residents of the village might now be infinitely better off in terms of clean water, instant light and waste removal, but other aspects have definitely declined. Today, there is still a flourishing primary school but there is no shop, no post office and following the closure of the Butchers Arms in the 1990s, just one pub which forms part of a hotel. In comparison, in the 1930s, there were a wealth of services – for some, leaving the village may have been desirable but was certainly not essential.

> *"Ampney as a village was nearly self sufficient. Gearings had a shop and a bakery and where*

Pinks is now, that was the village cider press. Your grandad would take apples down there and they would be pressed. He would pay them something, not much, and get it back in cider. There was a cobbler your for shoes and blacksmiths, not for shoeing horses although they could, but for metal work. Peter Sterry was the miller and he was also the taxi service, at first the taxi was a pony and trap and I can remember Granny Herbert being taken to town by him with all these rabbits to sell, but later he upgraded to a motor car. You could get petrol in the village although in the war that was rationed, I think it was four coupons for a two gallon tin. There was an estate yard with a saw mill in there run by a traction engine. The saw mill belonged to the Cripps but there were little smallholdings who shared machinery. Allotment lane was allotments all the way along and everyone grew their own vegetables. What is the car park near the school used to be the school gardens, no one needed to buy vegetables. You couldn't get everything in the village and so there were two buses in the day to Cirencester, Dingles and Tommy Littles. The main thing for us that we needed was parafin from Georgie Rows. Things also came into the village; butchers at least weekly and there was a big store 'Edwards' at Poulton, you gave them a list for what you wanted to buy the next week and it was ready for you."

Utilities and facilities

Today with public services becoming less and less visible some aspects of 1930s Ampney sound almost incredible.

> *"There was a village nurse at the bottom of the village, it's still called Nurses' Cottage. She was like a community nurse, she delivered babies and if anyone had dressings that needed changing she would do that. There was a police station and I can remember several policeman: Jackson, Penville and one called Wyatt. They didn't have cars, just bikes and a whistle. The other person I remember was Barnes, he was the carpenter and the undertaker. So you had everything from beginning to end."*

The services have vanished but the house names hint at what was once there.

Outbreak

∽

Dad was only seven years old at the outbreak of war but even so recognised that the countryside around him was changing.

> *"I wasn't aware there was going to be a war but I was aware there was something going on, I knew summat was happening. I can remember your grandad taking me up to Cerney aerodrome, that had just been completed and watching the planes come in, I know now that they were Hawker Harts and South Cerney turned into the Central Flying School."*

The image of a family sitting around the radio on the 3rd September 1939 listening to Neville Chamberlain describing the Nazi invasion of Poland and then finishing his broadcast with the words, 'and that consequently, this

Wally's wall where Dad played football as the beginning of the Second World War was announced.

country is at war with Germany', has been depicted on the screen hundreds of times. Dad, not realising that in future years this scene would be iconic, was occupied differently.

> *"Your grandad was quite a keen radio fan, so we always had a good radio. Gran and Grandad they would have heard the speech on the radio but I didn't. I can remember where I was though when Gran called me in to tell me, I was playing with a ball up against Wally's wall."*

The announcement was followed with what became known as the phoney war, the country took action even though nothing then seemed to happen immediately. But in 1940 the war began in earnest.

"Blackouts started almost immediately. I can remember tape being put on the windows of the school, put on all the windows to stop them shattering. We didn't have air raid shelters like they did in the bigger towns, the only air raid shelter I can remember was the one at the Regal Cinema in Ciren. There were bombs though, some of the first bombs of the war round here fell on what we call Tank Lane, just past the Harnhill turn. The tank's long gone now."

Evacuation

On the 1st September, two days before the official start of the biggest conflict the world has ever seen the British Government implemented 'Operation Pied Piper'. This involved the movement of around three million people and brought a word into everyday use: 'evacuees'. The scale of the operation was amazing even though the code name was questionable. In 1939, parents of city children were told of the importance of sending the children to the countryside but there was no suggestion that, unlike the children lured away by the Piper of Hamlyn, they would not return.

The children who came to Ampney Crucis came in the main from East Ham in London. Evacuees played a big part in the lives of my dad and grandparents, their two evacuees Peter and Doreen remained regular visitors throughout their lives. Peter often stayed with my grandparents sleeping in the same room he had shared with Dad. Dad remembers their arrival clearly.

"The evacuees came right at the start of the war, they were all in the village hall with labels round their necks, just like you see in the films, and your gran picked out Doreen. There was her and her sister Violet, Violet went back earlier in the war. Then because we only had the two bedrooms, Doreen later in the war was rehoused with the Puffetts. A family called the Nuttings had two evacuees, Peter and another Doreen and for some reason Peter came to live with us, I would say from December 1943, I don't know what happened to that other Doreen. Peter stayed with us and he didn't go back until the end of the war. A lot of the evacuees went back when the bombing stopped, and then it started again."

The following is a story I hadn't heard before from either Dad or Gran.

"There were petrol tanks at the top of Hunts Hill and there was lorries all the way down the village. That was one of the tragedies at that time, there was an evacuee by the name of Malcolm Hamilton that was evacuated with Granny Herbert at Hilcot End. I can remember it well… well I was there. We were on the wall, we'd been down to the church on a Sunday and we were running on the top of the wall, by the football field. There were military lorries parked on the opposite side of the road and

then another one come down the road and squashed Malcolm against the wall. Mike Harris's grandad, he pulled the wall down on the field side but it was too late, I suppose he was already dead."

I wondered who told Malcolm's mother Winifred that her son had been killed in the place where she had sent him for safety and came home only to be buried. I also wondered how Granny Herbert coped with the death of yet another child.

The war effort

∽

If you were not in the Army, Airforce or Navy there was an expectation that you would still be part of the war effort and the most well known aspect was the Home Guard. Although 'Dad's Army' are now figures of fun, these villagers, many of whom had already experienced four years of war, were an important part of the defence plan if the threatened invasion took place. A few years ago Dad bought a folder of photographs and histories of the men from Ampney Crucis who had fought in the First World War. Men from this small Cotswold village fought in France, Belgium, Turkey, India, Egypt and Mesopotamia. The pages show men in their uniforms posed in studios, the photos that would have stood on family sideboards. Dad remembers many of the soldiers who returned as older men.

> *"Frank Day's story, I think that is incredible, he was injured at Mons in the first month of the*

war and then he was kept by the Germans, but he had tetanus then pneumonia and pleurisy then eventually he came back to England and had to have his leg amputated. I remember Frank well. Archie Day, how he survived I don't know, he joined up in 1915, went to Mesopotamia where he was severely wounded. So he was taken to Bombay to a hospital then was back to Cairo and rejoined his regiment then within a year he was back in hospital in Bombay with a heart attack, he finally got back here in 1919."

But now just over twenty years after they had taken off their uniforms for what they must have thought was the last time, there was another job to do.

"The Home Guard was formed early in the war and most of them were in the first war, Don Underwood's father and Mike Harris's grandfather had both been sergeants. They all used to parade on a Sunday morning by the beech tree near the school and all of us kids used to go along and watch them. Peter Stoworthy, he was a dispatch rider, and us kids in the scouts we were supposed to be runners. They used to practise throwing hand grenades along here at the Marys and just where you turn to Ashbrook there was a concrete pillbox. I think there was a general plan of what should happen if there had been an

invasion, whether it would have worked or not is another thing.

The other main group was the special constables, and your grandad was a special. There were about twenty of them and a Colonel Mackay was in charge. They used to walk round at night to see all the blackouts were in place and generally help the permanent policeman who were at the police station opposite the cemetery. It wasn't that there was a lot of crime, really it was just another activity for people. Mind you, your grandad did apprehend a murderer. There was a bit of a domestic, along at Ranbury just before you get to Poulton, a husband and a lodger were both hedge cutting and the husband killed the lodger with one of the hedging hooks. Well, Frank Day, who had one leg, he was permanently at the police station, he reported it and the regular policeman and your grandad went out and got this fellow. What happened to him afterwards I don't know. He got hung I 'spect."

Rationing

With less than a third of the country's food being produced at home and Nazi forces targeting the merchant shipping bringing the other two thirds, rationing was introduced almost immediately. Petrol was restricted to business and essential use from 1939 and from early 1940 food rationing began. The typical rations of the time have inspired various television shows. Modern day families are shown endeavouring to produce meals using weekly rations of two ounces of butter and one ounce of cheese or making Christmas dinner from offal. But these programmes in general portray the experience of people in the towns and cities. Dad's memories wouldn't make particularly good TV.

> *"We weren't affected by rationing very much though I suppose essentials like sugar and tea were, the things we couldn't make or grow. We all had big gardens*

and allotments, there were thousands of rabbits and nearly everybody had a pig. Your grandad and Ernie Goodall used to have a pig between them, it was kept at your grandads and there were hens in houses as well. Everybody had a gun. People having guns wasn't about arming the population it was just standard – shooting rabbits and anything else they could find. Sometimes soldiers from the parachute regiments or the glider regiments would be having an exercise nearby and they might ask for extra food. There was one occasion when one of them knocked on the door and asked if they could have some eggs but when he went to get them he found that the others had already raided the hen house."

Christmas was also far more recognisable than the TV programmes depict.

"We didn't have trees, they didn't really get going until well after the war but we still had Christmas dinner and some presents. Not many presents, but I can remember hanging up a pillowcase. Christmas dinner was usually a pheasant that your grandad had come across. There were pantomimes as well, just village ones, everyone came to our house for rehearsals because your gran was a really good seamstress and made all the costumes for the pantomimes and other village productions."

Coupons on clothing meant that 'make do and mend' was a necessity rather than a fashion, but one way to acquire material was barter. My grandparents resourcefully combined their skills as a handyman and seamstress.

> *"Your grandad used to do up bikes and as they were the main form of transport that could be traded. The Red Lion pub at Ampney St Mary was a sort of trading centre and so he used to take a bike down there and he would swap it for a parachute. Then your gran would make the parachute into whatever was needed at the time, shirts blouses, aprons, I remember Vera Golding's wedding dress being made out of a parachute."*

School

∽

Despite the war, children of the village still needed to be educated but this was complicated by the arrival of the evacuees.

"Ampney school wasn't just the school for Ampney it was for all the other villages as well. Places like Barnsley, they had schools but they were shut down in the '20s, it was the start of bigger schools in one place, they were extending Ampney school even before I started there in about 1937. The time I remember most was when the evacuees came. It seemed like there was hundreds of them, I think the school must have trebled in size. To start with, the evacuees were educated separately, they had come with their own teachers, four of them I think, and they had a headmaster called Ingersall. I always remember him because he brought a proper cinema projector

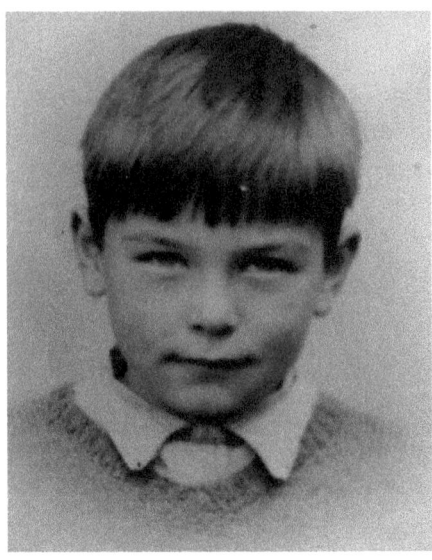

A schoolboy Dad at the start of the war.

with him that could do feature films. Unfortunately Ampney School's own headmaster found out that this Ingersall was of German extraction and reported him. So that was the end of him at Ampney, he was interned on the Isle of Man for the rest of the war. But he did leave behind the projector.

Being there were so many evacuees the teachers knew they couldn't keep us separate and have us in school five days a week – there wasn't the room. They had the idea that we would go three days one week and two days the next and the evacuees had it when we weren't there – so the education was pretty poor. After the first year they decided it didn't work and so they mixed us up together. Of course, they still didn't have enough rooms to do that so they had to take on the village hall and that was used as a classroom."

Not only did school have to carry on, so did school dinners. This was brought about by a brilliant piece of wartime organisation. The British Restaurants, originally known by the less attractive name of 'Community Feeding Centres', were staffed by the Women's Voluntary Service. They provided cheap, off the ration meals, for working people as well as delivering hot meals to schools.

"School dinners used to come out from the British restaurant in Ciren. The food came out in big double skinned metal containers filled with hot water so they were like big flasks. We had proper hot food, two courses every day. I can't remember many of the things they served up but I can remember what I didn't like, some sort of boiled fish with potato, that was awful. The puddings were often steamed puddings, spotted dick that sort of thing and were also issued with a free third of a pint of milk. The milk carried on for years, right up until the 1970s when Maggie Thatcher stopped it."

As to what was actually taught, the national curriculum was at least sixty years away and so lessons were very much up to the individual teachers with their own interests and knowledge gaps but with the war being a daily influence.

> *"We didn't have anything like English, we just had reading and writing lessons, there was nothing like science, I don't think the teachers knew anything about science. Everything was a bit of a mix, we had gardening because of the 'Dig for Victory' campaign, the garden was in what's now a car park by the old council houses. Bees, we were taught about bees because a teacher by the name of Skinner, he had bees and we had a glass beehive in one of the*

The original Ampney School now a private house. The current school was built in the 1960s.

classrooms. You could see the bees and the tube went outside so they could get in and out. There was quite a bit of education on the radio, I can't remember exactly what it was we had had to listen to but I remember Dave Poole and Frank Parsons had to carry this radio round the classrooms. Then there was the religious stuff, the vicar came on a Friday at nine, I remember we had a family called, I think, the Barons who were Catholic and so they were sent home on Fridays.

Best part of school was later on when you were about twelve and you went into Ciren into the council school to do woodwork. We had to cycle in so we went in on our bikes and did woodwork on Monday afternoon. Sometimes we escaped and went to the pictures but unless you passed the eleven plus and went to grammar school it was hopeless really. I left school when I was thirteen because when the evacuees were here, if your birthday was between terms you left the term before. So my birthday was at Easter which meant I left at the Christmas. It was just at the period I think when they didn't want the majority too well educated; they just expected you to go to work on the farm. I was on the farm at Ashbrook estate on my fourteenth birthday. Even before that you could be on the farm in school time. There was this blue ticket system, the farmers had these blue forms and they would tick it once for each day you worked for them. You could work for up to thirty days on the farm in term time – no wonder we never learnt much, we weren't really there."

War news

∽

Now, with international news available to us twenty-four hours a day, even a conflict involving a few hundred people in a small area of one country can be viewed on the screens in our lives. In contrast, when the world was last at war, there were only three sources of news for the general population: newspapers, the radio and cinema news. I did wonder if the news of the war itself would reach Ampney Crucis but it did.

"Yes, we knew what was going on, very much so, in particular I would say we knew more about what was going on after about 1942 or maybe it was because I can remember it better because I was a bit older. Mostly the information came from radio and papers, your grandad had the Daily Express *in them days. There was always big maps showing what was ever going on. It wouldn't always have*

been the exact truth because they would have been trying to keep up the morale of the country especially early in the war when there was the Battle of Britain and the Blitz. You couldn't get news about people so much, one of your Gran's nieces, Maisie, was living in Bath at the time and that was bombed really heavily in 1942. Gran said you could see the glow at night but it was weeks before they knew if Maisie was still alive. I can remember Dunkirk, I wasn't quite aware how serious it was because I would only have been around eight years old. When it was D-Day and later, Arnhem I was older and I can remember hearing the planes going over. When it was D-Day the planes woke us up, the planes for Arnhem came over later, about nine or ten o'clock in the morning. And then there was just the build up of military vehicles, American ones in particular. We would look out for these as the soldiers would sometimes throw sweets out of the back of the truck for us. Then one day they were gone, all moved to the south coast to join the invasion."

Crash

∽

The Cotswolds might have been a safer place than London or the other big cities but there was still intense military activity. In a twelve mile radius of Cirencester there were around thirty military establishments including more than a dozen RAF camps, four major airfields, US and British military hospitals and the headquarters of the Danish Special Operations Executive where Danes were trained in espionage and sabotage. The combined presence of these establishments meant the Cotswold countryside was the scene of numerous accidents and incidents as well as being a target for German bombers.

"There were always plane crashes, they were a regular occurrence, 'specially with the Oxfords. Sometimes might be one every couple of weeks but sometimes there might be a couple of months and we

wouldn't have one. I remember a Sunday morning being along at the beech tree, and from there you could hear these engines, they would flare up when they went wrong and then there would be a bang. One day, we heard this roar and an Anson had crashed just behind Hilcot End and there were nine on there. Apparently it was a plane taking chaps on leave and was coming into South Cerney aerodrome and the tail fell off before the main plane crashed. Jockey Lafford from the village was at a base in East Anglia at the time and he actually spun a coin to come home on that plane but lost the toss, and good job too. I remember there was a big elm tree at the bottom of Hilcot End at that time. I don't know whether he jumped but this man certainly came out before the plane crashed and you could see his imprint for weeks, you could actually see where his fingers had gone into the subsoil. So crashes were a regular occurrence, but not always fatalities – some just skimmed along the ground and that was that."

Some of the incidents like this would have been simply mechanical failure but others were definitely not.

"It would have been 1941 or 1942, so I would have been nine or ten years old. A German plane came across the village and machine-gunned it quite heavily. He was machine-gunning the field in front

of our house where there were a load of sheep but he didn't hit any. He blew several windows out around the village, the Butchers Arms sign had a big hole in it and the tin bath on the back of Chris Bowles house, that was riddled with bullets. But eventually the plane was shot down by a Hurricane coming up from Kemble and it crashed at Coates."

Fun and games

∽

In the 1940s the population was focused on Germany and Japan being the enemy and the idea of 'stranger danger' didn't occur to anyone until 1970s. This meant that the children of Ampney and all the surrounding villages had the open countryside as a giant unsupervised playground. Prior to the war the main risks were broken bones through falls or drowning in rivers, the war added some far more interesting hazards in the environment.

> *"We spent most of our time collecting surplus ammunition. It could be anything, someone even found a cannon shell that hadn't exploded. When there were exercises going on with the paratroops and Home Guard, we would all be on the lookout for the ammunition blanks. When we got them we would put them in a curtain rail and hit them with a nail and hammer to make them go off, which they*

did with a terrific bang. Another thing we would have would be thunder flashes, we had them by the boxful. Dave Poole and me had a load of these at this old place called Granny Freeman's, she had been an old lady who stood at her door all dressed in black but when she died it just became derelict. Before they knocked it down you could get into the cellar and Dave Poole and me we had piled up several boxes of thunder flashes and set them off trying to blow it up, I don't really know why. We would have been locked up now."

Not only did they now have the materials for entertaining themselves, sometimes they could have a show.

"The Home Guard used to get along here at the Marys practising hand grenade throwing. I can remember sitting on the wall watching this with Dave Poole and Tone Truman, they were phosphorus grenades. As soon as they had finished they retired to the Butchers Arms and of course us kids we were straight over there to see what had happened to these grenades. We found one that hadn't gone off but we knew these weren't just going to go bang, they were more dangerous than that, so we got Mike Harris's grandad out from the Butchers. He was still in uniform and he tried to set it off by throwing stones at it but he kept missing. So as he kept missing he

kept getting closer and eventually he hit it and it went off, but by then he was so close he got covered in this phosphorus. I can see him now running towards Hilcot End throwing his jacket off because it was burning holes in it."

The end

∽

The end of the Second World War is another one of those scenes where the footage focuses on the towns. The most familiar films are that of the crowds in the Mall in London, the Royal family on the balcony of Buckingham Palace with Winston Churchill, and street parties between rows of terraced houses. The end of the war was no less welcomed by families in rural Ampney Crucis but the celebrations were less elaborate.

> *"Yes, I remember the end of the war, well the European war, that was finished but the Japanese war in the Far East that was still going on. In terms of a celebration of VE Day – yes there was a big bonfire where the Pleydells are now. There weren't fireworks but the RAF from Cerney bought a load of flares down. I can't remember an actual party as such because rationing was still very much in force.*

The Pleydells estate was once Pleydell's field where the villagers celebrated VE Day.

We hadn't been affected that much but when the war ended bread went on rationing which it hadn't been before so that made a big difference. Also the lease lend from America was over and so everything was just that bit more difficult. I can't remember another celebration for VJ Day when the war in the Far East finished, I think everyone was just relieved it was over. But for the us kids, although we didn't really realise it at the time, it was the end of a lot of excitement."

After the end

∼

So the war finished and rural England returned to rural activities but Gran realised that opportunities needed to be created if the future was going to be different for her son.

> *"So at the end of the war I was down on the Ashbrook Estate. I'd gone there straight from school. Within a few months I was an apprentice carpenter and that's what I was doing when the war finished. I was always good at making things, I once made a timer system to turn on the lights in Grandad's hen house from an old alarm clock, a block of wood, a switch and a mousetrap. The hens needed light in the winter months but that meant going up and down to the hen houses in the pitch black so this did it from the house. Grandad sent in a drawing of it to the* Smallholder *magazine and it won a*

five pound prize. I did stuff in the scouts as well, the scouts were a big thing and I was in it until until after the end of the war. I got my King's Scout award just after the war.

So I wanted to make things rather than work on a farm and I was really lucky that my mum could afford a hundred pounds for me to be an apprentice carpenter otherwise I would have just stayed on at Ashbrook. A hundred pounds was a huge amount then, we got some from the Pleydell fund and I got twenty pounds from them for some tools. I only got ten bob (fifty pence), a week as an apprentice but after six months I got a pound a week because I already knew so many of the basics. Although I did the apprenticeship I don't think it meant that much to me at the time, it lasted five years and when I got the indentures, the paperwork you got when you had completed the apprenticeship, I don't think I even opened them.

My apprenticeship finished on the Friday and then it was about a week later I got called up into the army, I got called up originally when I was eighteen but if you were an apprentice it was deferred like it was for the few who were at university. Really that done me good, I was a bit older than majority of all the ones who went at eighteen. I think it was because I was older I was the only one who became an NCO even though some of the ones I was with went to the

*Left: Dad at the start of his National Service.
Right: On board HMS* Forth.

grammar school. Plus if I had went in at eighteen I would have been in Korea but that stopped in 1953. I'm not sure they knew what to do with us then. Norman Poole went in the same day as me, he was still only eighteen and he came knocking on our door the night before and said, 'You're going in the army tomorrow aren't you Harold?' and I said yes and he said, 'Can I come with you because I've never been on a train.' He finished up in Germany but I went to Malta – that was a much better job. Even in the army my carpentry came in useful. I was in the Mediterranean on a ship called HMS Forth. *A call came over the radio for me and I thought oh, what have I done now, but the officer*

Pulling down a Nissen hut in reverse.

wanted to know if I had ever built a Nissen hut which was a building that came in a standard kit. I said, 'No, but I've pulled plenty down.' The officer said, 'Well Stevens, I imagine it's just the same but in reverse, go and get your tools.'"

A new start

Mum and Dad met by chance at a cricket match in the early 1950s when she was staying with a friend. Mum was a nurse from North Yorkshire and the Cotswolds looked and sounded very different to her home. Today Ampney Crucis has elements of the picture postcard about it, but in post war Gloucestershire tourists were very thin on the ground. Ampney was very much a working agricultural village and Mum described how different it looked then.

> *"What I remember about the village when I first came here was that it was very muddy everywhere especially at Dudley Corner and down the street. There was a farm across the road so there were always animals coming past, sheep and cows, sometimes they would get in the garden. Tractors were going up and down the road all the time and*

brought all the mud. In the lanes there were just thousands of rabbits, droves of them running up the sides of the road, that was before someone brought in myxomatosis. Something that used to really make me mad was the water running out. The water we had wasn't mains water it was pumped up from the winterwell in Ampney Park which is where Ampney stream starts. The water went into a tank and then pumped up again to the village. There was this man and he was supposed to look after the pump but he would fill the engine up with diesel on a Friday, leave it running but by Sunday dinner time it would run out of fuel and so up here the water just ran out because we were at the end of the village up the hill. The Cripps, who were much lower down, they always had water!"

Like many newly-weds of the time, Mum began married life in her mother-in-law's house. Gran and Grandad's cottage had two bedrooms, a tiny kitchen and an outside toilet. This would have been standard for the time but would still have been cramped. Their own home was a priority but required another tenant to move out. By the 1950s this was a rarer event, retired workers were staying in their cottages and so moves could very much be a case of 'dead man's shoes'. Today, renting has become an industry in itself with agents, references deposits and detailed contracts. In the village at that time, with the

Cripps still the owners of much of the land and properties, the system was simpler. You were somebody from the village who needed a home and the Cripps' family had lots of homes. However the estate was far less wealthy than it had been and many of the cottages were in a state of disrepair verging on derelict. So, instead of paying a high rent for a cottage that had been newly decorated with the latest kitchen equipment and smart bathroom, you paid no rent at all on the understanding that if you wanted to improve your living conditions it was up to you to renovate and repair at your own expense.

But you still needed one of the homes to be free. Mum could recall the day a place became available.

"I remember Harold coming in one day really happy and saying 'Death has smiled on us!' which was awful really but it meant there was a cottage free so we were really pleased. We moved up to 49 Hilcot End as soon as we could. It was in a real state when we got there, the jackdaws had been building in the chimneys for years and all the nests had fallen through onto the floor. There were so many sticks piled up in there that we couldn't get the kitchen door open. It had a very old kitchen and in the corner was one of those great old fashioned coppers that had a fire underneath it for heating water. It was a great big hexaganol thing and I

Mum and Dad, April 1955.

just looked at it and thought what am I going to do with that? For cooking we had an electric cooker and we did buy a little fridge just to keep the milk cool. When we had lived with Gran her kitchen was cold and the stone meant she didn't need a fridge, especially as the milkman came round nearly every day. We didn't get a freezer until we moved back to Ampney to the new bungalow your dad built. That's when we got a phone as well, before that we would have to borrow one as there were one or two people who had them at that time. When I was expecting Heather and Maureen we had to go round to the Len and Ivy Gwinnett to use their phone. We used to get other things like potatoes from people in the village if we hadn't got enough in our own garden, everybody just paid in cash for everything and kept the money at home. Dad used to go to this old cottage for a bag of potatoes, the place was nearly falling down but they had no end of money. There was this Smiths Crisps tin and Dad said that when they opened it the pound notes and ten shilling notes were packed in so tightly that they used to jump out.

Keeping warm wasn't easy, there wasn't any central heating and so we had open fires and there wasn't any sort of proper bathroom so we had to manage with a tin bath. It was really cold in winter and I remember when Maureen wasn't very well we used this electric blanket to keep her warm. Then the electric bill came in and it was eight pounds and I just thought, however are we going to pay this? But we did."

The cottage at Hilcot end was a semi-detached. Mum and Dad lived on one side at number 49 with, by 1959, my sisters Maureen and Heather. At number 50 were the Clack family: Anne, Tony and their sons Peter and Toby. Within thirty years these two cottages that housed a total of eight people were knocked together to form one large house. This was then extended and a swimming pool added. It then became the holiday retreat of an MP representing Oldham near Manchester. Michael Meacher was a cabinet minister in the Labour Party in the 1990s who appeared to have no problem in disapproving of second home owners while having several himself…

Heading into the modern age with added snow

∾

By the 1960s Dad's carpentry skills had extended to building and he decided that, rather than spending money on someone else's property, home ownership was the way ahead. However, as there were no houses available to buy, he and his friend and one day business partner Ted began to build their homes in their spare time – a set of semi-detached bungalows. Planning permission in the 1960s was a slightly less formal affair than it was today.

> *"When we wanted to build the bungalows they were the first new private houses to be built since the war. Some council houses had been built after the First World War and then a few more down School Lane in the 1950s. But private individuals were limited both by the sewerage system or lack of it and also the*

fact that the Cripps owned the land and for many years they didn't need to sell it. Then the sewerage came and also the Cripps were selling off parts of the estate so we took our chance and went to Gloucester to see the planners as Cirencester didn't have any planning officers then. We saw a junior planning officer called David Lee who had just come out of the Airforce. I suppose we were talking about National Service and I could see he wanted to help us. He went through all the planning rules and said we would have to apply but that it might take quite a few months but we wanted to start because we needed the light evenings after work. I told him all this and so he found an old envelope and wrote on the back, 'I give H Stevens and E Brain permission to build two bungalows subject to planning.' So having that to get going, we started building the bungalows. I was still working for the building firm Camerons and so we were working on the site in the evenings when it was light and in the winter when it was dark we were making things for the bungalows. We spent a lot of time making all the window frames ourselves as it was too expensive to buy them."

As Dad began to think about building the bungalows, the whole country began to change and in lots of ways it seemed for the better.

Heading into the modern age with added snow

A birthday party in a new modern home.

"*I think the end of the 1950s and the beginning of the 1960s were the best time we have had. There was no unemployment, jobs were easy to come by and it seemed that everyone's living standards were going up. People began to have luxuries like television in their own homes. We had our first television when we were living at Hilcot End and it cost eighty pounds. At the time I was earning about eight pounds a week from my job with Camerons but I was doing lots of extra work as well in my own time as eight pounds was still less than my army pay of eleven pounds. There were all these ninety-five per cent grants for people to have bathrooms and toilets, flush toilets were put into in the houses and in general there seemed to be plenty of local authority money about. Definitely winter road clearance was better than it was now and yet we had more snow."*

Snow clearance is something that is currently a source of newspaper headlines and annoyance for a short period of time every few years. But shortly after Dad and Mum moved into the bungalow in the early 1960s it became a national issue for months on end as a winter arrived by which Dad still measures all winters.

"1963 was a really terrible winter, the snow and freezing went on for ten weeks. I was working for Camerons and they shut the whole firm down which was probably about a hundred employees, we all had to go round to the labour exchange as we had been laid off. All our cards were sent to the labour exchange and we had to wait ten days for any money at all and then it was only thirty shillings. When I went to collect my money there was a note on my cards saying the manager wanted to see me and he said, 'You've been working' and I said, 'Yes I

have, I've got a family to keep.' He said, 'If you take the thirty shillings we will prosecute,' and I said, 'Well you know what you can do with your thirty shillings!' But it was all fine, because I was foreman, after a couple of weeks they got me to go back to look after the apprentices because they weren't allowed to lay them off. I managed very well, I had a big job on for a confectioners in Ciren making a display cabinet. Camerons didn't start again until the 10th of March.

Mum, Heather and Maureen dwarfed in their own driveway by the winter of 1963.

It wasn't just the snow and cold that made it so bad, it was the wind as well. At the bungalow we had a rayburn cooker in the kitchen which was going all night, but in the morning there was a snow drift in front of it in the kitchen. The snow was that fine and being driven by this gale force wind that it blew it under the back door. Lots of houses, including Ted's, they just froze up solid so you couldn't get any water. Ted and I used to go round the village because we discovered that most of the houses had lead or galvanised underground pipes and we had an electric welder. We found that we could put one end on the stop tap in the street and one in the house and thaw it out with the electric – we did quite well out of that…"

In the late 1960s Dad, who was still working for Camerons, and Ted who was an electrician with Williams and Ford, decided that they could do quite well out of their own projects and joined forces to become Stevens and Brain Ltd. They worked together for the next thirty years.

The great escape – cars for all

From the 1960s onwards a growing disposable income meant that on top of home comforts such as bathrooms rather than tin baths, there was money available for one of the main changes of the times; the arrival of cars in the village for the general population rather than just the wealthy.

> *"In the war there weren't really any cars about, petrol was rationed and it was again for a few months in the mid '50s because of the Suez crisis. Cripps' agent he had the first one that I can remember, your grandad he had an Austin Seven, one with a canvas roof and then in the '60s he had one of the first Minis. He didn't take a test, there weren't any tests until the '50s, I got mine when I was doing National Service. The first one I had was a Standard 9 car, it cost me eighty pounds. Back then, the main way to*

get a second hand car was the adverts in the Wilts and Glos. Standard and you had to get it as quick as possible or the cars would be gone. I was working opposite the Wilts and Glos. one time and I knew that a bloke would come and stand outside who did the proofreading. I managed to persuade him to show me the proof copy, wrote down the details of the advert and got the car. Another one I had was a post office van, we used to go up to Yorkshire visiting your Mum's family in that and it was a really long journey in the '60s because there weren't the bypasses that there are now, you had to drive through towns rather than round them. There weren't seatbelts at the time, they didn't come in until much later and so we used to put a mattress in the back of this van for Maureen and Heather to sit on. Couldn't do that now."

Last thoughts

In some ways the village is now unrecognisable to the village of 1939, a lack of agricultural mud and farm animals being driven through it being one of the biggest differences. The farmyard opposite Mum and Dad's house became one of many barn conversions in the area and Dudley Farm, where Mr Robinson became one of the first local farmers to use a milking machine, is now a small estate of houses. The Cripps family slowly vanished from the village, Ampney Park and Waterton House were sold off and eventually Park Farm, the last family home of the Cripps, had new owners. But the tradition of being part of the village remained, they still own some land but sold the cricket pitch and the football pitch to the village. Cricket matches are still a feature of the village but Ampney United football team kicked its last ball many years ago.

Although the population may not have increased substantially the number of houses certainly has and many of them were built by Dad and his partner Ted. Later they specialised in renovating older buildings, including the oldest one – the church. Even now, noticeboards, church doors, gates and benches are being produced by Dad for use in the village. So there have been physical changes, but these are nothing compared to the social changes. The 1939 record shows a village of, in the main, manual workers. The list includes general labourers, stockmen, cowmen, gardeners, stone masons and the occasional mechanic. There were one or two teachers, a retired police constable and a butler but in general, the men of 1939 worked with their hands and their wives were at home carrying out what the record described as 'Unpaid domestic duties'. Now residents are more likely to be living next to a stockbroker

Worker's cottages are now picture postcard residences.

than a stockman and their house, even if it may have started life as a council house, is far more likely to be theirs, or at least theirs and the banks.

It has also become common to say that community life has been lost in the villages and no one knows who their neighbours are any more. It may be true to say that villagers do not know everyone in the village in the way that the pre-war villagers did. Dad once described how, one evening, he and Grandad sat down and counted all the dogs in the Ampney Crucis. I cannot imagine that we will ever return to that level of knowledge of individual households. But Mum and Dad's neighbours can often be found in Dad's

Still carpentering in retirement, Dad with the new church gate. A gift from Jack Edwards, a Second World War pilot 1918–1998.

shed, there is still a Women's Institute, touring film clubs, bring and buy sales and an annual village fete.

So the Ampney Crucis which has existed since Roman times and has survived through Norman invasion, civil war, and two world wars will doubtless survive for many more years. But I do doubt that anyone, outside a small corner of south Gloucestershire, will ever be able to spell it.

Afterword

*John Buck Lloyd, Philip Munday, Reginald Poole and
Alexander Scott Ronald. Ampney Crucis men who, between
1939 and 1945, gave their lives for their country.*